SPECIALS!

Hinduism

Mary Green

Folens Publishers

Acknowledgements

The authors and publisher would like to thank the following for permission to reproduce photographs and other material:

Pages 12, 32	The Bhaktivedanta Book Trust International
Page 14a, b	Mark Edwards/Still Pictures
Page 25a	Illustrated London News Picture Library
Page 25b	Popperfoto
Page 40	Ann & Bury Peerless

Folens allows photocopying of pages marked 'copiable page' for educational use, providing that this use is within the confines of the purchasing institution. Copiable pages should not be declared in any return in respect of any photocopying licence.

Folens books are protected by international copyright laws. All rights are reserved. The copyright of all materials in this book, except where otherwise stated, remains the property of the publisher and author. No part of this publication may be reproduced, stored in a retrieval system, or transmitted, in any form or by any means, for whatever purpose, without the written permission of Folens Limited.

This resource may be used in a variety of ways. However, it is not intended that teachers or children should write directly into the book itself.

Mary Green hereby asserts her moral rights to be identified as the author of this work in accordance with the Copyright, Designs and Patents Act 1988.

Editor: Edward Rippeth   Illustrations: Tony O'Donnell of Graham-Cameron Illustration
Layout artist: Suzanne Ward   Cover design: John Hawkins of Design for Marketing
Cover image: The Hutchison Library

© 1997 Folens Limited, on behalf of the author.
Every effort has been made to contact copyright holders of material used in this book. If any have been overlooked, we will be pleased to make any necessary arrangements.

British Library Cataloguing in Publication Data. A catalogue record for this book is available from the British Library.

First published 1997 by Folens Limited, Dunstable and Dublin.
Folens Limited, Albert House, Apex Business Centre, Boscombe Road, Dunstable, LU5 4RL, England.

ISBN 1 85276 786-3

Contents

Introduction 4
Teachers' notes 5–7

Beliefs and values
Beginnings 1 and 2 8–9
The first Hindu gods 10
The Hindu Cycle of Life 1 and 2 11–12
Samsara 13
The caste system 14

Signs and symbols
Signs and symbols 15
Names 16
Symbols and worship 17
Gods and symbols 1 and 2 18–19

Key figures
Brahma 20
Vishnu 21
Shiva 22
Shakti 23
The Hindu gods' family tree 24
Mahatma Gandhi 25
Gandhi and the Harijans 26

Places of worship
The great temples 27
The Ganges 28
Hindu shrines 29
Puja 30

Daily life and rituals
Hindu food 31
Vegetarians 32
Women and Hinduism 33
Pilgrims 34

Special times
Hindu festivals 35
Divali 36
Holi 37
Birth and early childhood 38
A Hindu marriage 39
A Hindu funeral 40

Writings
The Ramayana 1 and 2 41–42
Ganesha and the monster king 1 and 2 43–44
Krishna and Narkasur 1 and 2 45–46

Lotus flower game 47
Glossary 48

Introduction

The activity sheets in this book are designed to make complex ideas accessible to pupils with learning difficulties in Years 7–9 following a course in Hinduism. They are meant to supplement existing courses and are not a course in themselves.

Although the book is concerned with Hinduism it should be used within a broad context so that a range of religions are addressed. Pupils should develop a respect for those who do not share the same religious beliefs and should also be made aware that there are beliefs outside religions.

Those who enter secondary school with a history of learning difficulties, usually manifested in limited literacy skills, can bring a profound sense of failure with them. Its effect takes many forms and goes far beyond the academic loss experienced, but, as teachers know, such pupils are not necessarily below average intelligence. The activity sheets, therefore, cover a range of levels and include extension activities. Although they follow a common format, outlined below, they can be adapted to meet individual needs.

Activity sheets

Each activity sheet is divided into four linked sections:

Background
This gives a brief outline of the context and can be referred to while students undertake the activities. Pupils with few reading skills can read the background with a partner and discuss its meaning.

Activities
These are the main tasks related to the topic and may include paired or group discussion, practical or written tasks or refer to sources, the glossary or particular concepts.

Key words
All key words are highlighted in bold and can be found in the glossary.

Find out
A greater degree of independence is needed to complete these extension activities. They usually involve investigative work and simple study skills, such as using an atlas and library research. From time to time more sophisticated recording of data using, for example, interview skills is required and pupils are encouraged to work in pairs or groups. A maximum of four pupils in a group is suggested since larger groups can discourage some pupils from participating.

Teachers' notes

The notes are designed to give guidance on teaching strategies and differentiation. They indicate:
- What all pupils should complete and understand.
- What those with fewer difficulties should progress towards.
- When those with greater difficulties would need increased intervention.

Glossary

The key words on each activity sheet can be found in the glossary. This should be copied and made available for regular use, since many of the concepts and terms in Hinduism are complex.

Additional resources

The teacher will need to provide atlases, scissors, glue, colouring pencils, card, pins and note paper, for occasional use.

Teachers may also wish to provide a selection of books which cover the Ramayana, the Mahabharata and the Bhagavad Gita. Stories such as those included in this book are often popular as cartoons in India. Pupils could look at different presentations of the same tales and use these simple stories as an introduction to more developed literature.

Teachers' notes

BELIEFS AND VALUES
Beginnings 1 and 2   *pages 8–9*
- After the activity, all children should be able to answer (however simply) the questions, what are religions? How did they begin? They should be able to explain the pictures they have drawn for their charts. (This should help with subsequent activities on '*Signs* and *Symbols*', page 15).
- Those with few difficulties should be able to complete the extension work. This will require some simple research and organisational skills.
- Those who experience the greatest difficulties should work with a partner to talk through their ideas and complete the chart. They could then focus on using the glossary and understanding the key words.

The First Hindu gods   *page 10*
- All pupils should have an understanding of Indralock and the relationship between the Aryan gods and the natural world. They should be able to relate this to the nature gods discussed in the previous activity sheets.
- Some pupils should be able to complete the extension work and in particular recognise the implication that the 'thousand-eyed' Indra sees everything and everywhere. They should also be able to discuss the ways in which goddesses and female spirits are presented.
- Those with the greatest difficulty should be able to place the gods appropriately on the collage. The illustrations on the activity sheet can be cut out and used and it may be necessary to dispense with the gods' Hindu names if they are too complex to remember.

The Hindu Cycle of Life 1 and 2   *pages 11–12*
- The first activity sheet should be done by all pupils so that they understand what a cycle is and recognise the Hindu Cycle of Life. They also need to know what the gods represent and understand that the cycle is continuous.
- Those who progress well can do the second activity sheet in conjunction with the activity sheets 'Brahma', 'Vishnu' and 'Shiva' and apply their understanding to picture A. They should also recognise that Shiva as the Cosmic Dancer is not simply the Destroyer but keeps the cycle moving.
- Those experiencing the greatest difficulty should focus on making the cardboard circle and understanding what each god represents.

Samsara   *page 13*
- The main aim is for pupils to understand the key words samsara, karma and dharma. Exchanging ideas and arriving at a consensus should help to do this. They should also try to look carefully at controversial issues related to this belief. As far as possible all pupils need to tackle the discussion point about the position of the poor and sick.
- Those completing the extension work should acquire a fuller understanding of dharma as a moral code and its relationship to samsara and moksha.
- Pupils experiencing the greatest difficulty who may not be able to complete all the activities should focus on the concept of samsara, using the illustrations on the activity sheet as an aid to understanding.

The caste system   *page 14*
- All pupils should be able to identify the difference between photographs A and B and as far as possible relate this to the caste system.
- Some might understand that a belief in reincarnation can reinforce the idea that one's place in life is fixed and can be changed only through rebirth. These pupils should be able to complete the extension work and may wish to do further work on Mahatma Gandhi.
- Those with greatest difficulties should focus on noting the differences between the photographs in terms of poverty and wealth.

SIGNS AND SYMBOLS
Signs and Symbols   *page 15*
This activity sheet is intended for pupils who have difficulty in understanding what symbols are. Other pupils should not need to do. Once the main activities have been completed satisfactorily pupils should attempt the extension work. This asks them to demonstrate their understanding and it may be necessary for further practice to be given.

Names   *page 16*
Each pupil could discover the meaning and origin of his/her own name. The teacher may therefore need to provide appropriate reference books.
- All pupils need to understand that words have origins and may have hidden meanings. Identifying the meaning and origin of their own names helps this understanding. It also helps introduce Hindu symbols which are numerous and complex.
- Those who cope easily can move quickly to the extension work. The names listed are all Hindu gods. References to them can be found in the glossary. However it may be appropriate for some pupils to do their own library research first.
- Those experiencing greater difficulty should focus on their own name and work with a partner to produce a card.

Symbols and worship   *page 17*
- All pupils should try to grasp the concept that a central belief of Hinduism is that god is in everything and that the senses are important in heightening awareness. They should be able to classify the symbols according to the senses.
- The OM is an abstract concept. Some may understand it as a basic sound or rhythm. These pupils can do the investigative work suggested.
- Those experiencing the greatest difficulty should focus on one sense at a time, identifying the symbols to match.

Gods and symbols 1 and 2   *pages 18–19*
- These activity sheets can be done in conjunction with activity pages 8–9 and 17.
- All pupils need to grasp the idea that Hindu gods and goddesses have particular qualities.
- Those who can understand that these qualities are regarded as part of a greater whole should be able to do the extension work.
- Others who have difficulty moving beyond the first activity should make up their own symbols for the gods represented. They could then compare their ideas with those shown in the pictures.

KEY FIGURES
Brahma, Vishnu, Shiva, Shakti   *pages 20–23*
These four activity sheets can be used together or separately. They should be increased to A3 size.
- All pupils need to acquire some knowledge about the principal gods and their relationship to each other. The Hindu belief that Brahma, Vishnu and Shiva – Creator, Preserver, Destroyer – are really one, may need to be reinforced.
- Some pupils may be able to make a topic card for each god, referring to the page 23, '*The Hindu Gods' family tree*'. They could

Teachers' notes

combine the completed topic cards to make a zigzag folder. This can be used as a resource in the classroom.
- Those experiencing greater difficulty could either identify the symbols for each god and label them as suggested or focus on one god only, providing greater information. In either case they should work with a partner and read and discuss the background together.

The Hindu gods' family tree   *page 24*
- This can be used as a separate activity sheet or in conjunction with 'Brahma', 'Vishnu', 'Shiva', 'Shakti'.
- All pupils should understand what a family tree is and complete the main activities to demonstrate they understand the relationships.
- Those pupils who identify the family relationships easily need not write them up but can use the information for work on Brahma, Vishnu and Shiva and to complete the extension work.

Mahatma Gandhi   *page 25*
- By comparing photographs A and B, all pupils should identify the difference in Gandhi's age, appearance and demeanour. Encourage them to ask why he has changed and the teacher can relate this to the beliefs Gandhi developed. His popularity was due to his opposition to British rule, belief in non-violent protest, his dedication to the people and his capacity to follow his dharma.
- As far as possible all pupils should discuss the issue of non-violent protest. Those experiencing difficulties should work with a partner.
- Pupils with fewer difficulties should gather information on Gandhi's early years in South Africa to understand more fully how he developed his beliefs.

Gandhi and the Harijans   *page 26*
- Gandhi's condemnation of the dalits' treatment needs to be understood by all pupils. This should inform them when they compile a set of beliefs.
- Some pupils might be able to complete a short study of Gandhi's work. They should do the extension activities, referring to pages 13 and 24 to help them.
- Pupils experiencing difficulties should focus on compiling a set of beliefs, if possible, unaided, without necessarily moving to a discussion of dharma.

PLACES OF WORSHIP
The Great Temples   *page 27*
- All pupils should understand both the sacred nature of the temple and its life as a community. They can be made aware of this by observing all the features in the illustration.
- Those experiencing fewer difficulties can undertake a comparison of British and Indian temples, keeping the above points in mind.
- Those experiencing greater difficulties should focus on the illustration and discuss its features in some depth. They may then wish to design their own illustration, showing the temple as a place of worship and community.

The Ganges   *page 28*
- All pupils need to see the Ganges as a place of worship and a place where Hindus believe they can be spiritually cleansed.
- Those who are coping well and wish to extend their work on the Ganges need to recognise that water has significance in many religions.
- Those with difficulties should concentrate on the story of how the Ganges was created. Other versions along with illustrations could also be made available to pupils. They should try to understand the sacred nature of the Ganges through the story.

Hindu shrines   *page 29*
- This activity sheet should be done in conjunction with page 17. All pupils should be able to understand the personal and individual nature of Hindu worship and the teacher may wish to emphasise this point.
- Pupils experiencing fewer difficulties could discover more about family shrines and could interview any practising Hindus in their school.
- Those experiencing greater difficulties should select symbols for the picture and explain their choices to the teacher who can then clarify any misconceptions.

Puja   *page 30*
Emphasise the personal nature of Hindu worship. The teacher may wish to read aloud the account of Mina performing puja.
- All pupils should work through this account is some way.
- Those who complete the series of drawings can complete the extension work. They need to recognise the common feelings which Hindus share, such as silent thoughts, peacefulness and comfort, and recognise that puja can be performed differently with different gods involved. Mina's choice is Saraswati because she is the goddess of learning.
- Those experiencing greater difficulties should read the account of puja with a partner, using the pictures on the activity sheet as a guide.

DAILY LIFE AND RITUALS
Hindu food   *page 31*
- All pupils need to understand that the cow is a sacred animal for Hindus, be able to select the appropriate dishes and set out a menu. Pupils' drawings should reflect the religious nature of the festival they choose. Whether or not pupils choose a recipe to cook will be left to the teacher's discretion.
- Some pupils should be able to research why the cow is sacred, how it is treated and also find out about Pongal, the cow festival. The activity sheet 'Hindu festivals' may be useful here.
- Those experiencing major difficulties should work with a partner to choose appropriate dishes for the menu and can use the pictures to organise a menu.

Vegetarians   *page 32*
- The relationship between being a vegetarian and regarding living things as sacred should be seen by all pupils as an important Hindu belief. They should be able to identify the meaning of A, seeing it as a religious painting with the soul (atman) present in both the animal and humans.
- Some pupils may recognise the 'godly' in everything. A discussion about the various reasons for being vegetarian should also be useful. This can be developed into a larger project.
- Those experiencing greater difficulties should work with a partner and try to locate the quality of the picture: restful, non-violent, with harmonious relationships between humans and animals, using the points under Activities as a guide. They should also be told that the cow and elephant are regarded as special animals.

Women and Hinduism   *page 33*
- All pupils should be made aware that the Hindu woman is at the centre of family life but may also have a role in the wider society, for example, the teacher may wish to discuss Indira Gandhi.
- Pupils experiencing few difficulties should complete the main activities and look at other roles within the family, noting any cultural differences between family life in Britain and India, and their implications for girls.

Teachers' notes

- Those with greater difficulties should work more slowly identifying Hindu women's duties in the home in the first instance. Comparisons can be made with the roles their mothers have (if they are not Hindu). It may also be useful to talk to any female Hindu teachers about their dual roles, if possible. Note also the similarity of women's roles across the world regardless of culture.

Pilgrims   *page 34*
- Identifying the places on the map and recognising their geographical position in India should be completed by all pupils. Atlases should be available.
- Some will be able to complete the diary alone and should concentrate on the extension work, particularly the life of a sadhu which requires library skills and can be undertaken in pairs.
- Others may need assistance completing the map, but should also attempt the diary, at least orally. Working with a partner they could write up their ideas later and illustrate their work.

SPECIAL TIMES
Hindu festivals   *page 35*
- All pupils should understand what a timeline is and be able to create symbols.
- Some can move on to extension work and use the information to write more detailed accounts of Hindu festivals. They will need to identify the Hindu calendar.
- Those who have difficulty understanding what a timeline is should begin by completing their own, running from birth to present day and locating importance personal dates. They should then attempt the Hindu festivals timeline with a partner.

Divali, Holi   *page 36–37*
- The teacher may wish to use these activity sheets together.
- All pupils need to recognise that Divali is the more religious of the two festivals and that 'light' is a symbol of goodness and hope. Holi, a Spring festival in which the god Krishna features, should be seen as a time to joke and play tricks. Comparisons can be made with Halloween and Guy Fawkes.
- Pupils coping well can do extended work on both festivals, making comparisons and referring to other main festivals.
- Those experiencing greater difficulties should focus on the nature of festivity through making Divali cards, rangoli patterns and identifying the religious nature of Divali. They can also note the features of Holi and colour the illustration in the spirit of Holi.

Birth and early childhood   *page 38*
- All pupils need to know that there are sixteen samskaras in Hinduism and that these are steps which help the soul on its way.
- Those with few difficulties should complete the activities and investigate the deeper meaning of each samskara. Some may wish to find out what the remaining ones are. They should, in any case, discover the meaning of the sacred thread.
- Those working at a slower pace should complete the matching exercise and place them in order as 'a stair' beginning at the first step. This should help to illustrate the movement towards heaven. They should then discuss each step with a partner and try to decide which they think are the most important.

A Hindu marriage   *page 39*
- The ritual and detail of a traditional Hindu marriage needs to be understood and it is therefore suggested that all pupils should complete the main activity.

- Some pupils can investigate the deeper significance of the rituals. They may also wish to discuss the advantages and disadvantages of arranged marriages and can compare the differences between traditional and non-traditional marriages.
- Those with greater difficulty should complete the main activity checking that they understand the vocabulary with a more able pupil. The glossary can also be used.

A Hindu funeral   *page 40*
- All pupils need to understand that the body is no longer important after death, only the soul. The teacher may also wish to discuss samsara and the significance of the soul again.
- The extract from the Mahabharata can be tackled by those who understand the main beliefs easily. Here, Yudishthira has gained moksha. They may also wish to find out more about a Hindu funeral in Britain. This can be done in conjunction with page 38.
- Those who find the photograph difficult to interpret should work with a partner. They should try to identify the coffin with flowers, pyre and temple in the background.

BOOKS, STORIES AND MYTHS
The Ramayana, Ganesha and the Monster King,
Krishna and Narkarsur   *pages 41–46*
- These activity sheets can be used in conjunction or separately, as the teacher wishes.
- All pupils should read the stories and understand the plots.
- Those with few difficulties need not complete the main activities and should move straight to the extension work which asks them to consider the meaning of the stories. They are largely about good overcoming evil but also convey other messages. Rama and Sita are presented as the perfect marriage partners, Ganesha as the remover of obstacles and Krishna as the defender of the world. The teacher may also wish to provide more detailed versions and descriptive extracts. The Ramayana is a particularly rich source.
- Those with greater difficulties should read the story with a partner, complete the sequencing or multiple-choice activity together and should try to identify the main characters and if possible the main themes.

Lotus flower game   *page 47*
Rules
A game to reinforce key words. Enlarge to A3 size if necessary.
A game for two players
Tokens and dice will be needed.
1. Cut out the key word answer sheet and place it face down on the table.
2. Throw the dice to decide who starts. The highest number begins first.
3. One throw per player unless a six is thrown, which allows an extra throw.
4. Players should try to identify as many key words as they can. Players who answer correctly have an extra throw.
5. The winner is the first to reach the last square. The exact number must be thrown to finish,
6. The main object of the game is to collect and remember all the key words. This may take several games.

Beginnings 1

Background

What are religions? How did they begin?
Thousands of years ago people were unsure of the world around them. Although they were close to nature, they did not know where the rain came from, what caused storms or how plants grew. They believed that these mysteries must be the work of powerful gods. Beliefs such as this and the **worship** of nature gods were the beginning of **religions**.

There are clues about these early **deities** in our language. The names of the old gods can be found in certain days of the week.

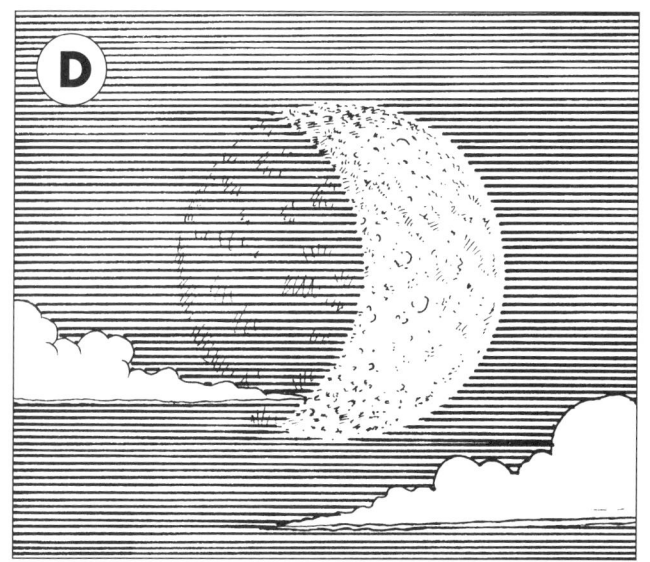

A

B

C

D

Beginnings 2

Activities

1. Draw up a chart like this and list the days of the week.
2. Match the descriptions to the pictures to work out what each day means.
3. Complete the chart by drawing your own pictures to match.

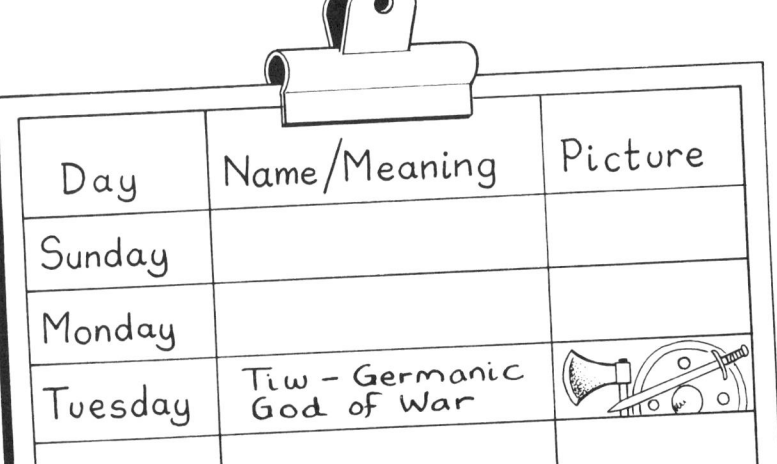

Day	Name/Meaning	Picture
Sunday		
Monday		
Tuesday	Tiw – Germanic God of War	

The source of all light and heat.

Brightens the night sky.

Freya, Norse goddess of fertility.

Tiw, a Germanic god of War.

A Roman festival named after the planet.

Woden, the Anglo-Saxon King of gods

Thor, the Norse god of Thunder.

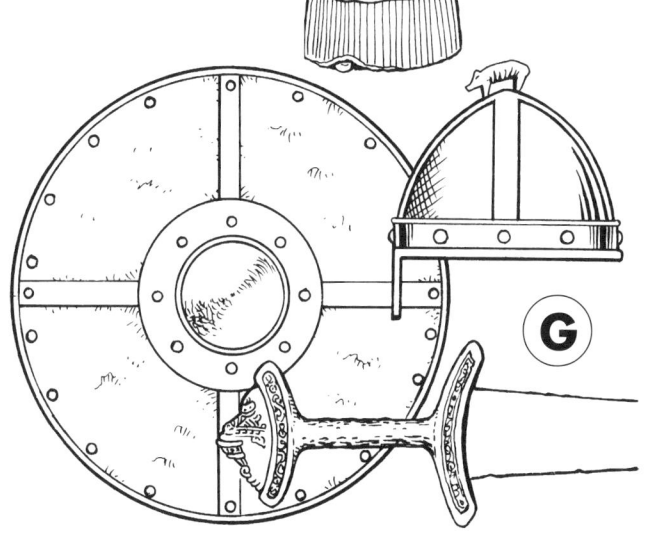

Key words

deity
religion
worship

Find out

- Choose one of the days of the week and find out as much as you can about its meaning. Write about it or discuss it with a partner.
- Find out where the names of these months come from: January, March, May.

The first Hindu gods

Background

Hinduism began thousands of years ago. The early religion belonged to a warrior tribe, the **Aryans**, who invaded the **Indus Valley**. They settled in what we now call the **Punjab**. Many of their gods were nature gods. Indra the warrior was the most powerful. He was the god of storm and heaven who ruled **Indralock**, the home of the gods.

Key words

Aryans
Hinduism
Indralock
Indus Valley
Kali
Punjab

Indra – warrior god of storm and heaven

Prithivi – earth mother

Surya – sun god

Vayu – wind god

Ushas – dawn goddess

Agni – fire god

Parjanya – rain god

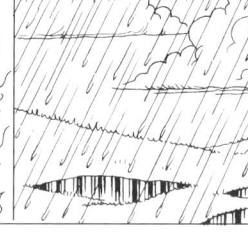

Asvins – twin heroes of heaven

Soma – the god of the magic soma plant

Vishnu – The Preserver who looks after everything

Aryan gods and goddesses

Activities

Work with a partner.
1. Design and draw a collage of Indralock.
2. Include the sky and upper heaven and the earth below.
3. Decide where you think each god should be and label it on the collage.

Find out

- On a map of India find:
  – the Indus Valley
  – the Punjab.
- Discuss with your partner:
  Indra has been called 'the thousand-eyed' and some paintings show him with many eyes.
  – What do you think this symbol means?
- Why do you think earth spirits are often shown as female?
  – Look at the Hindu goddess **Kali** on page 23. How is she different?

The Hindu Cycle of Life 1

Background

As **Hinduism** developed so did certain beliefs. The most important of these is the belief in life, death and **rebirth**. This is called **The Cycle of Life**. Hindus believe that three gods keep the cycle moving.

Brahma the Creator who makes life grow.
Vishnu the Preserver who looks after the universe.
Shiva the Destroyer who destroys life so that it can grow again.

Key words

Brahma
cycle
Cycle of Life
Hinduism
rebirth
Shiva
Vishnu

Activities

1. Make a circle from card.
2. Draw the three gods around the edge like this.
3. Put in arrows between them.
4. Write the 'Hindu Cycle of Life', 'Death' and 'Rebirth' in the middle.
5. Spin the card on a pin.
6. This will show you how the gods keep the cycle moving.
7. Work with a partner.
   Explain:
   – What a cycle is
   – the Hindu Cycle of Life.
8. Use a glossary if you need to.

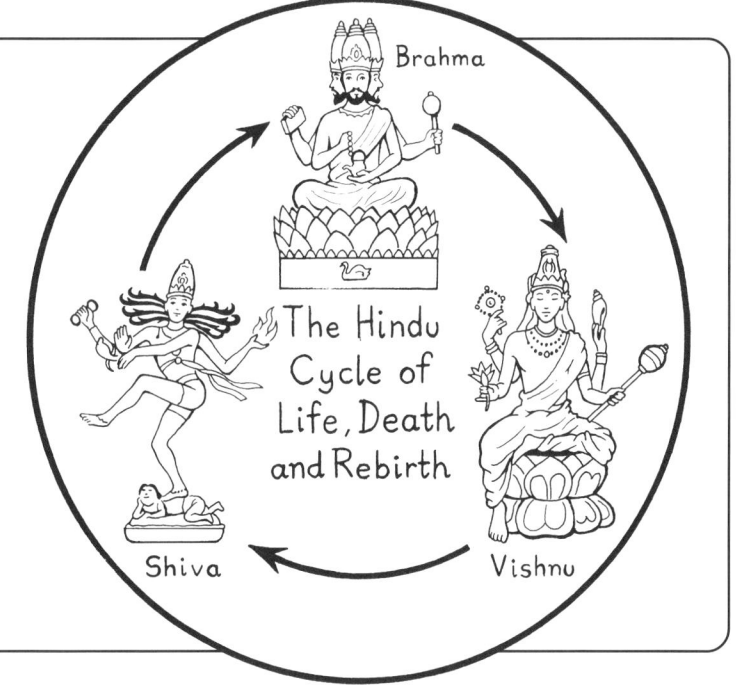

Find out

- There are many cycles in life. What is this cycle called?

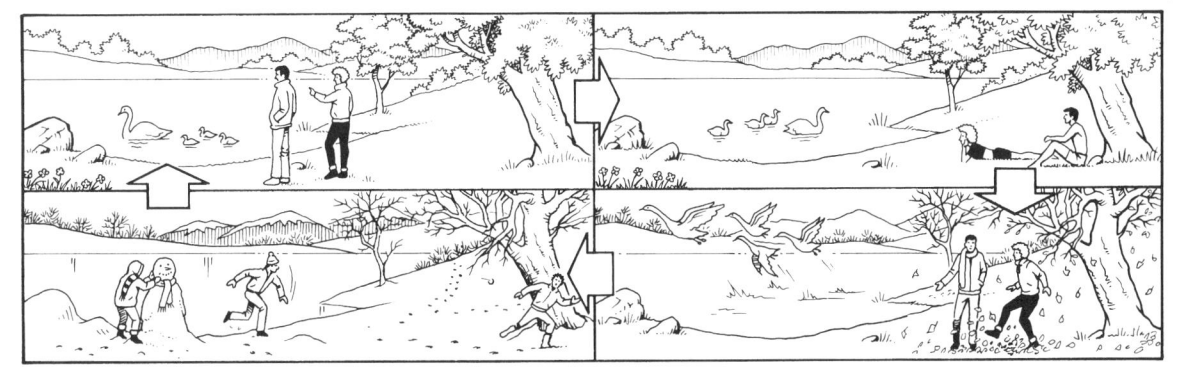

- Draw three more cycles. Think about your daily life.

The Hindu cycle of life 2

Background

In **Hinduism** everything is reborn – animals, humans, even the **universe** and the gods themselves.

Key words

Bhagavad Gita
Hinduism
universe

A

B

"Those who are born will die and the dead will be born again."

From the Bhagavad Gita.

Bhaktivedanta Book Trust International, © 1997

Activities

Work with a partner.
1. Look carefully at **A**.
2. What is happening in the picture?
3. Is there more than one person?

Now read B.
4. Talk about what it means.
5. How is it similar to **A**?
6. Write down your answers.

Find out

Now look at the activity sheet 'Hindu Cycle of Life 1' on page 11.
- Spin the card you made.
- How does the cycle link with the idea of Shiva as Lord of the Dance (see page 22)?
- Talk about your ideas with your partner.
- The **Bhagavad Gita** (Song of God) is one of the Hindu holy books. It gives advice through the story of Prince Arjuna.
- Try to find out more about it.

Samsara

Background

Samsara (or **reincarnation**) is the belief that when someone dies the **soul** (**atman**) passes out of the body into a new life. Hindus believe that everything is reincarnated including animals.

Dharma is the duty you have to others, what you should do for your family, friends and for yourself. What you become in the next life depends on **karma**, how well you have fulfilled your dharma. If you have led a bad life or failed in your dharma you may come back as an insect or animal.

Key words

atman
dharma
karma
moksha
reincarnation
samsara
soul

Activities

Work in pairs in a group of not more than six. Each pair could write these words in large letters on paper and cut them out.

samsara   karma   dharma

1. Decide together what each means and write it on the back, in your own words.
2. Put the words from the whole group in one pile.
3. Each pair should take it in turns to pick a word.
4. Read aloud the meaning.
5. In the group discuss whether or not you agree.
6. At the end the whole group should decide what the best meanings are.
7. Then check them in the glossary.

Find out

- What is **moksha**?
- Why do Hindus want to achieve it?
- If people are born poor or sick do you think it is fair to believe they must have behaved badly in the last life if this is believed?
- How might the poor and sick be treated if this is believed?

The caste system

Background

Traditional Hinduism stresses that you must accept your place in life. This can only be changed through **reincarnation** and the beginning of a new life. As a result there is a Hindu **caste** system. People are divided into upper and lower castes or **classes**. There is also another group outside the caste system. These are the poorest people. They are called **Dalits**.

Key words

- Brahmin
- caste
- class
- Dalit
- Gandhi
- Kshatriya
- reincarnation
- Shudra
- Vaishaya

Brahmins (priests)

Kshatriyas (rulers and generals)

Vaishayas (business people and skilled workers)

Dalits (the poorest)

Shudras (unskilled workers)

A

B

Activities

Look carefully at photos A and B.
1. How are they different?
2. Make at least three points.
3. How do they show the caste system?
4. How does the idea of reincarnation fit into the caste system?

Find out

- Read the activity sheet 'Gandhi and the Harijans' (page 26) and find out about what **Gandhi** did for the Dalits.

Signs and symbols

Background

Signs and **symbols** are pictures or objects that stand for something else. They can also be a mark or a movement. A wave of the hand is a sign of goodbye. Some symbols are harder to understand because they have deeper meanings. The curled snake is often used in medicine or health organisations.

Key words

sign
symbol

Find out

- Make up three symbols.
- Ask a friend to work out what they are.

World Health Organisation symbol

Activities

1. Work with a partner.
2. Look carefully at the signs and symbols below. How many do you know?
3. Find out what the others mean.

4. Now explain the symbols on a piece of paper.

5. When you have finished sign here _____ !

© Folens (copiable page)   SPECIALS! *Hinduism*

Names

Background

All names have meanings and most Hindu names have religious meanings. For example, Deepak is a boy's name and means 'light'. Pooja is a girl's name and means 'worship'.

Key words

Arjuna
Ganga
origin
Sita

Activities

1. Draw up a chart like this one.
2. List the first names of the pupils in your class.
3. Find out where they come from, what they mean and if they have a religious **origin**.
4. Make up a drawing to match the meaning of your own name. Turn this into a card.
5. Make a similar card for the next person below you on the list.
(If your name is last make a card for the person at the top of the list.)

Name	Meaning	Religion
Deepak	light	Hinduism
Peter	rock	Christianity
Pooja	worship	Hinduism

Find out

- Find out the meaning of these names and where they come from.
    Ganga
    Arjuna
    Sita

Symbols and worship

Background

Hindus believe that God is everywhere. This idea is expressed through **symbols** and one of the most important is the **OM**. It is a sound that represents **creation** and the rhythm of life. The five senses, touch, taste, smell, sight and hearing are also important in reminding Hindus that God is all around them. When they worship they give **offerings** which appeal to the senses.

The symbol of OM.

Key words

arti ceremony
arti lamp
creation
garland
incense
murti
offerings
OM
symbol

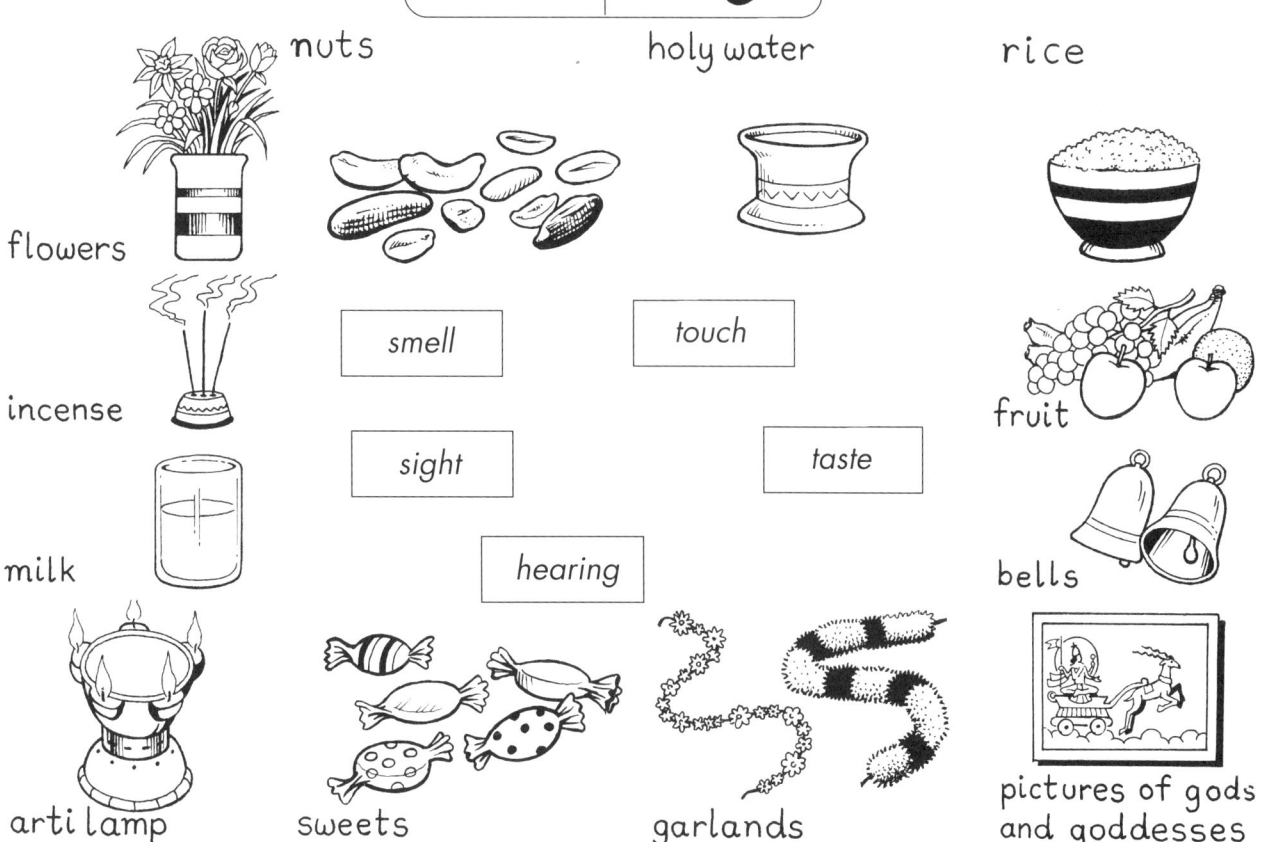

flowers — nuts — holy water — rice

incense — smell — touch — fruit

milk — sight — taste — bells

arti lamp — hearing — sweets — garlands — pictures of gods and goddesses

Activities

1. Look at the symbols above.
2. Match them to the senses which they will appeal to.
3. Remember, more than one sense may match each symbol.

Find out

- What is a **murti**?
- How is it involved in Hindu worship?
- What is the **arti ceremony**?
- Why do you think the flame is a symbol in many religions?

Gods and symbols 1

Background

Hindu gods can represent many things. They might stand for love, wisdom or good luck. Some represent nature but most represent a **quality**.

Key words

Hanuman
quality
symbol

Activities

Work with a partner.
1. Think of a special quality your partner has. It could be:
   - good at cooking
   - loves animals
   - always happy.
2. Whatever it is do not tell your partner.
3. Now design a symbol which sums up the quality.
4. Ask your partner to guess what it means.
5. Draw up a chart like the one below. With your partner, list the names of 12 people from your family and friends.
6. Make up a **symbol** to show one quality each person has.
7. Ask others in your class to guess what each symbol means.

Name	Symbol
1.	
2.	

Find out

- Who is **Hanuman**?
- What special quality does he have? Why?
- Find a story about Hanuman.

Gods and symbols 2

Background

Hindu gods and goddesses hold **symbols** in their hands to show what they represent. Whatever **qualities** they have, Hindus believe that all gods and goddesses are part of the **'Supreme One'**. To Hindus it does not matter which god you choose to **worship**.

Key words

Ganesha
Indra
Lakshmi
lotus flower
quality
Saraswati
Supreme One
symbol
worship

Indra

Saraswati

Ganesha

Lakshmi

1. goddess of music
2. god of storm
3. kind to children, gives them presents
4. goddess of riches and money
5. sometimes called the warrior god
6. holds an axe to remove obstacles
7. goddess of learning
8. sometimes called the goddess of the **lotus flower**
9. worshipped when a hard task has to be done
10. elephant god of wisdom and good luck

Activities

- Read the statements numbered 1 to 10.
- Look at the pictures of the four gods and the symbols they are carrying.
- Match each statement to one of the four gods.

Find out

- Why do you think there are so many Hindu gods?
- Read the background again to help you.
- Many gods and goddesses hold up one of their hands in front of them.
- Find out why.

Brahma

Background

Hindus believe that Lord **Brahma** created the **universe**. Although he is the Creator he is only part of the 'Supreme One'. The gods **Vishnu** and **Shiva** are the other parts. Like everything in the universe, Brahma himself is reborn through the **Cycle of Life**. He is often red or gold in colour and is drawn with four heads. These are to show that he has a mind which can think about all things. He also has four arms which hold **symbols** of religious books. These are **hymns**, **chants** and **verses** called the **Vedas**. Brahma is not often worshipped directly.

Key words

Brahma
chant
Cycle of Life
hymn
Shiva
symbol
universe
Vedas
verse
Vishnu

Activities

1. Make a topic card about Brahma.
2. Cut out the picture and stick it on strong card, then colour it in.
3. Label the symbols in the picture and explain what they mean.

Find out

- Use the activity sheet 'The Hindu gods' family tree' (page 24) and read the background again to write about Brahma.
- Check your work and correct any errors.
- Stick the final version on the back of the card.
- Put it on display for others to read.

Vishnu

Background

Once **Brahma** has begun the **Cycle of Life** again by recreating the universe, Vishnu looks after it. He is the Preserver of life. Paintings and statues often show him with a large snake or riding a holy creature, half man, half bird called **Garuda**. He also holds a **conch** shell. These were blown as horns at the start of battle.

It is believed that Vishnu comes down to earth in different forms to fight demons and keep the power of the gods safe. Sometimes he is Prince **Rama** or **Krishna** the wise man or an animal. He has ten of these forms. They are called **avatars** or **incarnations**.

Key words

avatar
Brahma
conch
discus
Garuda
incarnation
Krishna
mace
Rama
Vishnu

*Sometimes Vishnu carries a **mace** and a **discus**.*

Krishna likes to play tricks. He is also brave and helps humans in trouble.

Activities

Make a topic card about Vishnu and Krishna.

1. Cut out the pictures and stick them on strong card.
2. Colour Vishnu in yellow and Krishna blue.
3. Label the symbols in the pictures and explain what they could mean.
4. Use the glossary to help you.

Find out

- Use the activity sheet 'The Hindu gods' family tree' (page 24) and read the background again to write about Vishnu.
- Check your work and correct any errors.
- Stick the final version on the back of the card.
- Put it on display for others to read.

Shiva

Background

Shiva is the Destroyer. He is white or yellow with a blue throat, often wears a **garland** of skulls and carries weapons. He is sometimes covered with ashes. He is surrounded by demons or **goblins** and also by fire, a **symbol** of destruction. However, Shiva is not only the Destroyer. Destruction clears the way for new life. Hindus believe he is the **Lord of the Dance** who keeps the **Cycle of Life** moving.

Key words

Cycle of Life
garland
goblin
hourglass
Lord of the Dance
Shiva
symbol

*In this picture, Shiva is dancing in a ring of fire. In one hand he carries a small drum. This makes the noise of 'truth'. It is shaped like an **hourglass** because Shiva is also the god of time. In another hand he holds fire. A third hand is often held in blessing which means protection. What do you think Shiva is crushing under his feet?*

Activities

Read the background and the caption.
1. Make a topic card about Shiva.
2. Cut out the pictures and stick them on strong card, then colour them in.
3. Label the symbols and explain what they mean.

Find out

- Use the activity sheet 'The Hindu gods' family tree' (page 24) and read the background again to write about Shiva.
- Check your work and correct any errors.
- Stick the final version on the back of the card.
- Put it on display for others to read.

Shakti

Background

Shakti is the most important female goddess. She has many names and many forms. As **Durga** she is the warrior goddess of protection who has ten arms. She usually carries a sword, a shield, a spear, an axe, a discus and a bow and arrow and is often shown riding a lion. As **Kali** she is the goddess of death and the destroyer of time. She wears a necklace of skulls with the blood of monsters streaming from her. At other times Shakti is the gentle mother goddess **Uma** or **Parvati**, wife to **Shiva**. She carries a **lotus flower**. This can mean beauty or peace and protection.

Key words

Durga
lotus flower
Kali
Parvati
Shakti
Shiva
symbol
Uma

A

B

C

Activities

1. Decide which goddess is Durga, Kali and Uma.
2. Cut out the pictures and stick them on strong card.
3. Colour them in. Choose the best colours for each goddess.
4. Label the **symbols** in the pictures and explain what they mean.
5. Check your answers with a partner.

Find out

- Use the activity sheet 'The Hindu gods' family tree' (page 24) and read the Background again to write about the three goddesses.
- Check your work and correct any errors.
- Stick the final version on the back of the card.
- Put it on display for others to read.

© Folens (copiable page)   SPECIALS! *Hinduism*

The Hindu gods' family tree

Background

There are many Hindu gods. They are like a large community. Look carefully at the **family tree** below to see how some of them are related.

Keywords

Brahma
cosmic
Durga
Ganesha
Kali
Kartik
Krishna
Lakshmi
Nataraj
Parvati/
Uma
Rama
Sarasuati
Shakti
Shiva
Vishnu

Brahma
(Creator born from a golden egg in the oceans.)

Saraswati
(goddess of music and learning born from Brahma)

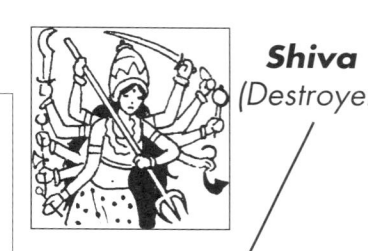

Vishnu (Preserver) = **Lakshmi** (goddess of riches.)

Prince **Rama**

Krishna

The Fish

The Tortoise

The Boar

Vishnu has five other forms

Shiva (Destroyer) — **Shakti**

Nataraj (cosmic dancer)

Durga (warrior goddess)

Kali (goddess of death)

Parvati or Uma (gentle mother goddess)

Kartik (god of war)

Ganesha (elephant god of wisdom and good luck)

KEY

= married

—— other form (incarnation)

--- son or daughter

Activities

Work with a partner.
1 Study the key and talk about:
 – who is married to whom
 – the two sides of Shiva.
 – how Kartik and Ganesha are related.
 – why Vishnu is different.
 – the three sides to Shakti.
2 Then write up your answers.

Find out

- Are Brahma and Saraswati similar in any ways to Adam and Eve in Christianity and Judaism?
- Try to find out what Vishnu's other forms are.

Mahatma Gandhi

Background

Mohandas Gandhi was a famous Hindu leader. He was called **Mahatma** by the people which means 'great soul'.

At the time Gandhi lived, India was ruled by the British. He felt his country should be free and he refused to obey British laws. Gandhi believed strongly in non-violent **protest** and went to prison for his beliefs.

Key words

Gandhi (Mohandas)
Mahatma
protest

A

B

Activities

Look at A and B and describe each photograph.
1. How has Gandhi changed?
2. Why do you think this is?
3. Why do you think Gandhi has so many followers?
4. Think of at least three points.

Find out

- Gandhi spent 21 years in South Africa before returning to India. What did he do there?
- How did it help to form his views? What does non-violent protest mean?
- Do you think it achieves more than violent protest?
- Explain your answer.

© Folens (copiable page)   SPECIALS! *Hinduism*

Gandhi and the Harijans

Background

Gandhi led a simple unselfish life. He believed that the **caste** system was wrong and helped those who were the poorest. These people were often called the '**Untouchables**'. They called themselves **Dalits** or '**oppressed**'. Gandhi gave them a new name, the **Harijans** which means 'children of god', and did the same poorly paid work as they did. In 1950 it became **illegal** to treat people as untouchable.

Key words

caste
Dalit
dharma
Gandhi
Harijan
illegal
oppressed
Untouchable

Activities

Gandhi had a set of beliefs that were very important to him.
Here are some:
- you should lead a simple life
- you should earn your own living
- you should not be afraid.

_____
_____
_____
_____

1. Add more of Gandhi's beliefs to the list.
2. Read the background on this activity sheet and 'Mahatma Gandhi' (page 25) again to help you.

> *'Do the work given to you according to your dharma.'*
>
> From the Bhagavad Gita
> (A holy Hindu book)

3. What do you think this means?
4. Use the Glossary if you need to.
5. How did Gandhi try to follow his **dharma**?

Find out

- Talk with a partner about the difference between:
  - Gandhi's view of the Dalits
  - the Dalits' view of themselves.
- How do Dalits live now?
- Do you think a change in the law has made life better for them?
- Explain your answer.

The great temples

Background

There are many great **temples** in India. **Varanasi** is a holy Hindu city which is built near the River **Ganges**. **Pilgrims** travel there to worship **Shiva** and wash themselves in the **sacred** river. The temples of Varanasi are looked after by hundreds of priests. They also look after animals which are used at **festivals** and keep stalls to sell offerings and religious pictures and statues. A Hindu temple is called a **mandir**.

Key words

festival	sacred
Ganges	Shiva
mandir	temple
pilgrim	Varanasi

Activities

1. Look carefully at the picture.
2. List all the things that are happening.

Find out

- Why is the shape of the temple important?
- Try to visit a Hindu temple in Britain.
- Note how it is different from temples in India.

The Ganges

Background

The Ganges is very special to Hindus. It is a **sacred** river. Many pilgrims visit the Ganges bringing flowers as **offerings**. They believe that bathing in the sacred water will wash away their sins.

A Hindu story tells how the Ganges was created. As the water poured down from heaven the god **Shiva** caught it in his hair stopping it from flooding the earth. Slowly the water flowed down the **Himalayan** mountains to become a river.

Key words

Himalayas
offerings
sacred
Shiva

Activities

Work with a partner.
1. Talk about why water is a special symbol to Hindus.
2. Draw three pictures below to show the story of the Ganges.
3. Write a sentence under each picture.

Find out

- Make a topic card on the Ganges.
- Find out:
  – where it is
  – what the goddess of the Ganges is called.
- Redraft the work you have already done.
- Think of another religion in which water is important. Say why.

Hindu shrines

Background

Hindu **temples** do not have to be large and grand. Many Hindus make their own **shrines**. These may be found at the roadside or at home. A family shrine will have a small statue or picture of a favourite god or gods surrounded by **symbols** and offerings.

Key words

Ganesha
shrine
symbol
temple

Activities

Look at the picture above.
1. It is the shrine of the Nandi family. It is for the elephant god **Ganesha** who symbolises good luck, wisdom and hard work.
2. Now look at the activity 'Symbols and worship' (page 17).
3. Choose a range of symbols to decorate the shrine.
4. Draw them in the best place on the picture and label them.
5. Explain your choice of symbols to a friend.

Find out

- Find out more about family shrines, using a library.
- Explain what a shrine means to a family.

© Folens (copiable page)   SPECIALS! *Hinduism*

Puja

Background

When Hindus **worship** their gods it is called **puja**. Mina is performing an act of puja. Read what she says.

Key words

arti lamp
arti tray
ghee
incense
meditate
offerings
prasad
puja
Saraswati
tikka mark
worship

*This is how I like to perform puja before I go to school. First I wash myself and then I wash the murti, which is the statue of **Saraswati**. She is my favourite goddess. I place a **tikka mark** on her forehead. The **arti tray** is placed in front of Saraswati. I make offerings of flowers, fruit, **ghee** and holy water and burn incense sticks. I light the **arti lamp** and ring the bell to let Saraswati know I am ready. My brother joins me and also makes offerings. We turn round three times to show that God is all around us. Then we pray or **meditate**. Afterwards we share some **prasad**.*

Activities

Work with a partner.
1. Make a series of small drawings to show how Mina performs puja.
2. Use the glossary to help you.
3. Label the drawings.
4. Take it in turns to explain them.

Find out

- Who is Saraswati?
- Why would Mina like her best?
- Puja may be performed in many different ways but the feelings will be the same for all Hindus.
- Try to explain what these are.

Hindu food

Background

One of the most **sacred** foods for Hindus is milk because it comes from the cow, a holy animal. Food containing milk is offered at **puja**, at festivals and other special times. It is also used a great deal in Indian cooking.

Key words

chapati
ghee
kheer
mango
puri
puja
raita
sacred

Chapatis
Mix flour and water slowly to make a dough. Cook in the oven.

Bengali kheer
Made with rice, milk, raisins, spices, sugar. Decorate with rose petals.

Mango aroma
You will need mangoes, milk, cream, coconut and almonds for this sweet.

Cucumber raita
A yoghurt dish with cucumber.

Puris
Bread made from flour and water and fried in **ghee**.

Chachumber salad
Use tomato and other vegetables, lemon juice, coriander and lettuce leaves.

Baigan masala
Steam and fry aubergines, masala spices and onion in ghee. Eat with bread.

Activities

1. Choose from the dishes above to make a menu. All dishes must contain milk or food made from milk. (You will need to check the key words in the glossary.)
2. Decorate your menu for a religious festival.

Find out

- Why is the cow so important? Use the library to help you.
- What is the cow festival called?
- What happens?
- Choose one of the recipes above. Make it at home or in school. (Always talk to your parents or teachers first about this.)

© Folens (copiable page)   SPECIALS! *Hinduism*

Vegetarian

Background

Many Hindus are **vegetarian**, although some eat meat. They believe that all living things are **sacred** and should not be harmed. This belief is called **ahimsa**.

Key words

ahimsa
vegetarian
sacred

From the Bhaktivedanta Book Trust International, © 1997

Activities

Work with a partner.
1. Look carefully at the picture.
2. Talk about:
   – what you think the people are doing.
   – what the people feel about the animals.
   – what is special about the people and animals.
   – how you know it is a religious picture.
3. Try to sum up what you think the picture means.
4. Now talk about your ideas with another group.

Find out

Work with a partner.
- Interview a Hindu who does not eat meat (visit a local temple or choose someone in your school).
- Interview a vegetarian who is not a Hindu.
- Find out from each one why they do not eat meat.
- How are their views the same and different?

Women and Hinduism

Background

Hindu women lead their lives in many different ways. This is to do with their **caste** and where they live. It also depends on how far they follow Hindu **traditions**.

Hinduism is not just a religion, it is a way of life with the family at its centre. All the family members have duties to each other but it is the women who keep the home running smoothly.

Key words

caste
tradition

We have two daughters and a son. I take care of the home and do the cooking. My two sisters help me to look after the children. I also prepare for festivals and special times.

As well as taking care of the family I teach my daughter how to perform puja and look after the family shrine. I also keep a record of the money we spend and control the family budget.

Activities

1. Record the duties these Hindu women have.
2. What other duties might they have?
3. Discuss with a partner how their lives are similar and different.

Find out

- Who was Indira Gandhi?
- In what way was her life different from most women?
- How is life for Hindu girls in Britain different from their mothers?
- What are Hindu men's family duties to their:
  – wife and children
  – parents and other relations?

Pilgrims

Background

Many Hindus make long journeys to important religious places. These are called **pilgrimages**. They visit holy cities and the sacred river Ganges wearing simple clothes and eating simple food.

Sadhus are Hindu holy men. Their lives are like one long pilgrimage.

Key words

Bengal
dharma
dharmasala
pilgrimage
sadhu

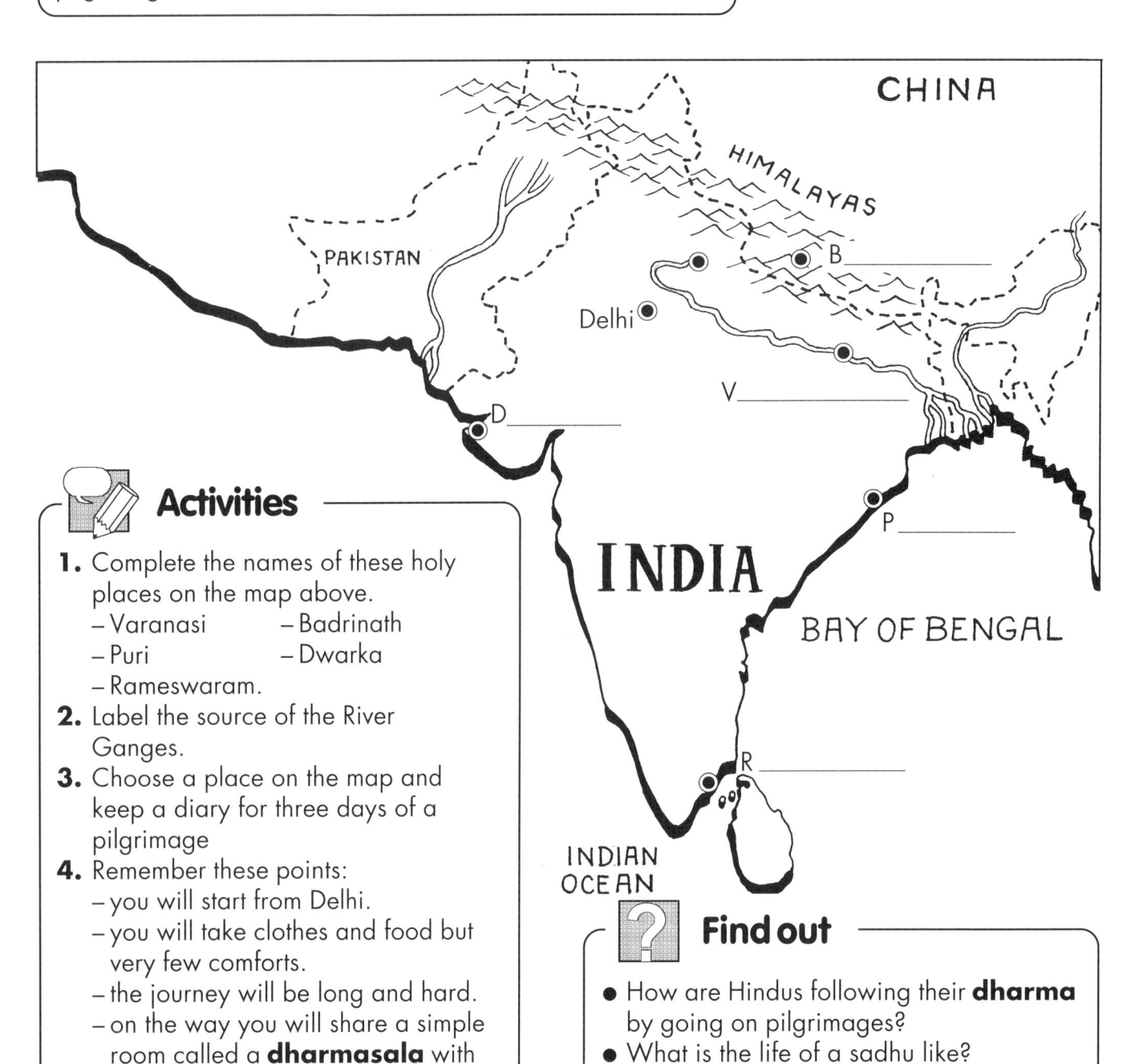

Activities

1. Complete the names of these holy places on the map above.
   – Varanasi   – Badrinath
   – Puri   – Dwarka
   – Rameswaram.
2. Label the source of the River Ganges.
3. Choose a place on the map and keep a diary for three days of a pilgrimage
4. Remember these points:
   – you will start from Delhi.
   – you will take clothes and food but very few comforts.
   – the journey will be long and hard.
   – on the way you will share a simple room called a **dharmasala** with other pilgrims.

Find out

- How are Hindus following their **dharma** by going on pilgrimages?
- What is the life of a sadhu like?
- Use the library to help you.

Hindu festivals

Background

Hindus love **festivals** and many are held throughout the year. Most festivals celebrate gods and goddesses.

Key words

The festivals are also listed in the glossary

Raksha Bandhan, held in August, the Indian wet season, when sisters give their brothers bracelets.

Pongal, the festival of the cow held in Southern India in January, the cool or winter season.

Janmashtami, Krishna's birthday, held in early Autumn, usually September.

Shivartri, held for the god Shiva in February, Winter or cool season.

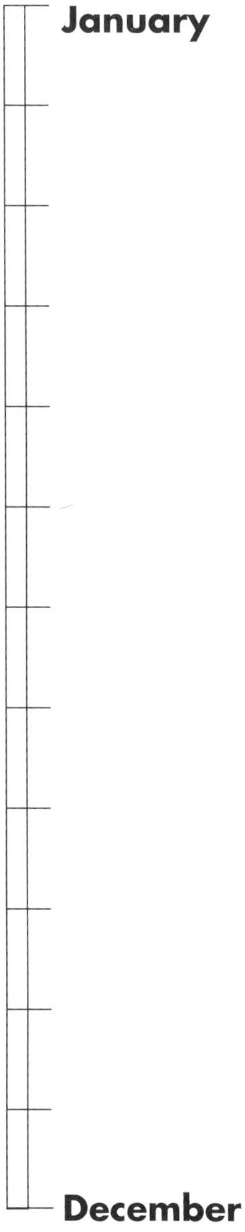

January

December

Divali, the festival of lights held in October, late Autumn.

Navaratri, held for the goddess Durga in September, late Autumn.

Rath Yatra, the chariot festival held in June, the rainy season.

Holi, Spring festival of love held in March.

Activities

1. Complete the months of the year on the timeline, then put the festival names in the correct places.
2. Draw a suitable symbol for each festival.

Find out

- What are the names of the Indian seasons?
- What is **Rama Naumi**?
- When is it held?
- When is the Hindu New Year, **Ugadi**?

© Folens (copiable page) SPECIALS! *Hinduism* 35

Divali

Background

Divali, the festival of lights begins just before the Hindu New Year. It is held in **Ashwin** – September/October – and lasts between three and five days.

There are many stories told at Divali. These change in different parts of India but most are about goodness overcoming evil. Light is the symbol of goodness and Divali means 'a row of lights'.

Key words

arti lamp
Ashwin
Divali
Ganesha
Krishna
Lakshmi
lotus flower
Rama
rangoli

Hundreds of lamps called **arti lamps** or divas are lit.	Divali cards are sent.	Fireworks are set off.	Sweets are made from milk, sugar and coconut.
Patterns called **rangoli** are drawn on the ground to welcome the gods.	Stories are told about **Rama**, **Krishna**, **Ganesha** and many other gods.		In Southern India **Lakshmi** is worshipped by those in business.

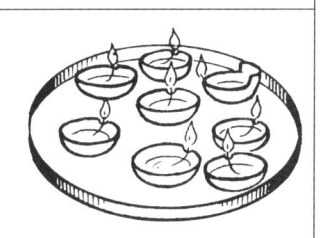

Activities

1. Make a Divali card in the shape of a lamp.
2. Decorate it with symbols of Divali.
3. Draw rangoli patterns.
4. Make flower shapes, such as the **lotus flower,** which means purity and beauty.

Find out

- In what way is Divali like the:
  - Christian festival Christmas?
  - Jewish festival, Hanukkah?
- What do these festivals mean?

Read the activity sheets on 'Ramayana' (page 41–42).

- Why do you think this story is popular at Divali?
- Enact a scene from the story with a group of friends.

Holi

Background

Holi begins on the day after the full moon in **Phalguna**, which usually falls in March. It is a Spring festival but there are many religious stories connected with it. Sometimes **Holika** is an evil spirit destroyed by fire. At other times she is a loyal sister who sacrifices herself on her brother's funeral **pyre**.

During Holi, bonfires are lit and there are many celebrations. On the second day, Colour Day, everyone is showered with coloured water and powder. This reminds people of the jokes Lord Krishna played when he was young.

Key words

Dassehra
Holika
Navaratri
Phalguna
pyre

Activities

Look at the picture and read the background.
1. List all the things that are happening.
2. Which god is being carried in the procession?

Find out

- Find a story about Krishna's childhood.
- Find one which tells about the mischief he gets into.
- Draw a series of cartoon pictures that tells the story.
- Who is worshipped at the festivals of **Navaratri** and **Dassehra**?

© Folens (copiable page)   SPECIALS! *Hinduism*

Birth and early childhood

Background

When a baby is born, Hindus believe it is the start of a new life that will lead to rebirth. To help the soul on its way there are sixteen steps taken called **samskaras**. Nine of these steps are in early childhood. The first begins before the birth.

Key words

horoscope
karma
sacred thread
samskara

At the naming ceremony food made from nuts and fruit is eaten.	The baby eats solid food.	The baby goes out in the sunlight for the first time.
The pregnant mother says holy verses to the baby.	The baby is washed and the holy OM is written in honey on the tongue.	The couple talk to a priest about the best time to become pregnant.
Around one year old the baby's head is shaved to remove bad **karma**.	The baby's ears are pierced.	The pregnant mother eats special food.

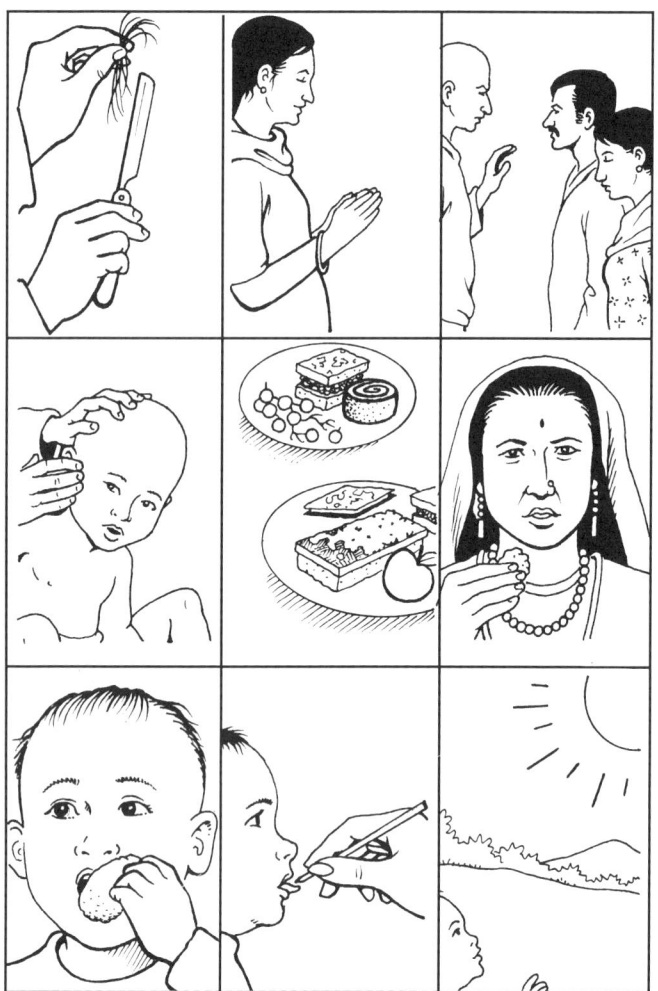

Activities

1. Cut out the pictures and the sentences and match them.
2. Now put them in the correct order.

Find out

- Why is the baby's first haircut important?
- Sometimes a Hindu priest will draw up the baby's **horoscope** at birth. Find out why.
- What does the tenth step or **sacred thread** mean?
- If there are Hindu children or teachers in your school interview them about samskaras.

A Hindu marriage

Background

Hindu **marriages** are often **arranged** in India and Britain. Many Hindus believe that partners should share the same background and **caste**.

Before the marriage takes place a **horoscope** is cast to fix the date and the marriage takes place at night when the **Pole Star** comes out. This means that promises made will be kept forever.

Key words

arranged marriage
caste
henna
horoscope
mandap
Pole Star
sari
tassel

*The bride and groom sit under a canopy called a **mandap.***

The bride wears:
- perfumed oil on her skin
- jewels on her head
- a red **sari** with gold thread
- gold bracelets
- silver anklets
- rings on her toes
- garlands of flowers
- patterns of **henna** on her feet and hands
- golden **tassels**.

The groom:
- is given food and money, symbols of good luck
- is dressed in white
- wears garlands of flowers
- wears golden tassels
- is joined to the bride by a white rope.

Activities

1. Read the information above.
2. Colour in and decorate the picture using the information. Draw on any missing items.
3. Label the picture.

Find out

- Why do the bride and groom take seven steps around the sacred fire?
- What part does holy water play?
- What does the symbol of the stone mean?
- What other religions have arranged marriages? Do you agree with this? Discuss in a group.

© Folens (copiable page)   SPECIALS! *Hinduism*

A Hindu funeral

Background

When Hindus die they are **cremated**. This is the sixteenth and final **samskara.** Hindus believe the body is no longer important, only the **soul** which will be reborn. The body is washed, wrapped in a new **shroud** and surrounded with flowers. Gold or silver is placed in the mouth. In India the coffin is taken to a **funeral pyre** for cremation. The eldest son stands by the pyre and prayers are said. Later the ashes are scattered on the **sacred** river Ganges.

Key words

cremation
funeral
Mahabharata
pyre
sacred
samskara
shroud
soul
Yudishthira

Activities

Look carefully at the picture.
1. Where do you think it was taken?
2. Explain:
   – What is happening
   – What will happen.
3. What is the building behind?
4. Do you think this is the **funeral** of someone rich or poor?
5. Explain how you know.

Find out

- Read this:

  > The sky became bright, Sweet airs began to blow. And Yudishthira, looking up, found himself surrounded by the gods. Well done! they cried.
  > *(The **Mahabharata**).*

- What do you think has happened to **Yudishthira**'s soul? Think carefully.
- What do you think happens to the ashes of Hindus if they are living in Britain? In what other ways would a Hindu funeral be different in Britain?
- Check your answers with a Hindu pupil or teacher.

The Ramayana 1

The great Rama lived in the city of Ayodhya with his wife Sita, ruling over a vast kingdom. Although he was a noble king he had enemies who plotted against him. He was forced to leave and, with his wife and brother Lakshmana, he escaped to the forest.

There they lived quietly and secretly until one day Ravana, the demon king, who had ten heads and twenty arms, swooped down from the heavens. He carried Sita away, taking her to the island of Lanka across the sea from India.

What was Rama to do? He did not know where Sita had gone. With the help of the monkey god, Hanuman, and Lakshmana he found out that she was being held in Ravana's fortress. All the monkeys of India then built a huge bridge which spanned the sea to Lanka.

A long battle began. The army of animals fought hard and many were lost. Finally, Rama's magic bow and arrow, made of fire and sunlight, struck the demon king and he was killed.

Sita and Rama returned to their kingdom where wonderful celebrations were held. Every year at Divali, the festival of lights, the story of Rama and Sita is remembered.

The Ramayana 2

Activity

1. Do this activity sheet after reading the **Ramayana** story.
Put the sentences in the correct order to tell the story.

Key words

Lakshmana
Lanka
Ramayana

He escapes to the forest with his wife Sita.	Hanuman the monkey god and Lakshmana help to track down the demon king.
Rama, Hanuman, **Lakshmana** and all the forest animals go into battle.	Ravana the demon king kidnaps Sita and takes her across the sea to **Lanka**.
Sita is rescued and they return to the kingdom.	The monkeys build a bridge to Lanka.
Wicked people plot to take over Rama's kingdom.	Rama uses his magic bow to kill Ravana.

Find out

- **Work with a partner.**
- What do you think the marriage of Rama and Sita means for Hindus?
- This is a description of what happens when Sita is kidnapped by Ravana. It comes from another story of the Ramayana. Read it together.
- Together make a collage or picture of the description.
- Try to find a longer story of the Ramayana. Read it with your partner.

> ... the lotus flower faded, the sun grew dark, the mountains wept in waterfalls ...
> the young deer shed tears and every creature lamented (cried).

Ganesha and the monster king 1

There was once a monster king called Gajamukha. He prayed every day and was very devoted. Lord Shiva was pleased and decided to grant Gajamukha a wish as a reward. This was just what the monster king wanted as he had only pretended to be holy. He would choose something which would give him power. So he wished that he could never be killed by any of the minor gods, any human nor any weapon.

His wish was granted.

Of course, Gajamukha now did as he pleased and nobody could do anything about it. He made everyone worship and obey him and punished those who refused. The gods were very unhappy. What could they do? Led by Indra, the god of storms, they visited Lord Shiva and his wife Parvati to ask for help.

Shiva took them to his temple. Written on the walls was the holy Hindu sign of OM. They all watched as Parvati stood in front of the sign and meditated. Slowly she began to change, taking the shape of an elephant. Suddenly out of the sign leapt their son, Ganesha, the elephant god.

Ganesha was set a special task – to kill Gajamukha. This was not easy. He fought and fought but no weapon he used worked against Gajamukha. At last Ganesha broke one of his own tusks and threw it at the monster king. It pierced Gajamukha's heart and he was instantly killed.

Ganesha had succeeded. He became the god who overcomes obstacles.

Ganesha and the monster king 2

Activities

1. Do this activity sheet after reading Ganesha and the monster king.
2. Finish the sentence for each picture to explain what is happening.
3. Cut out each picture and matching sentence.
4. Put them in the correct order to tell the story.

Key words

Gajamukha   **symbol**

Lord Shiva ...

Gajamukha pretends ...

Parvati ...

Shiva and Parvati ...

Ganesha cannot ...

Gajamukha wishes ...

Gajamukha is ...

Ganesha breaks ...

Find out

Work with a partner.

- Why do you think Ganesha is the **symbol** for overcoming obstacles?
- What does **Gajamukha** symbolise?
- Now write the story from Gajamujkha's point of view.
- Try to find the story of why Ganesha has an elephant head.

44   SPECIALS! *Hinduism*   © Folens (copiable page)

Krishna and Narkasur 1

Narkasur was a giant demon who lived in a terrible kingdom of dirt and squalor. Sometimes he would make expeditions in search of young women to take back to his kingdom. Although they screamed and shouted he would never set them free. So the women prayed to the god Vishnu for help. Hearing their prayers, Vishnu came down to earth as Lord Krishna, the wise man, to rescue them.

At the gates of Narkasur's kingdom was the great five-headed monster, Mura. To gain entrance Krishna had to kill the monster. A long and difficult battle followed before Mura was overcome.

Once inside Krishna tracked down Narkasur and attacked him on the spot. The huge giant fell to the ground, his vast body making a dreadful rumbling noise. As Narkasur lay close to death his mother appeared weeping. There was nothing she could do to save her son but she prayed that his death might bring happiness to others. Narkasur, in his last moments, was sorry for his actions and repeated his mother's words.

Thousands of women were set free. One of these was Lakshmi, Vishnu's wife, the goddess of wealth. She was now able to bring happiness and riches to all her followers.

Krishna and Narkasur 2

Activity

1. Do this activity sheet after reading Krishna and Narkasur. Tick the boxes to show the correct answer.
2. Then choose two characters to write about.

Key words

Krishna
Mura
Narkasur

Narkasur was a
- god ☐
- demon ☐
- goddess ☐

Narkasur was often
- happy ☐
- good ☐
- cruel ☐

Mura had
- five heads ☐
- five arms ☐
- five wings ☐

Narkasur's mother was
- sad ☐
- rich ☐
- angry ☐

Narkasur lived
- in heaven ☐
- with Krishna ☐
- on earth ☐

Lord Krishna was also
- Vishnu ☐
- Mura ☐
- Lakshmi ☐

Lord Krishna
- rescued Mura ☐
- rescued the women ☐
- rescued Narkasur's mother ☐

Lakshmi was
- Mura's wife ☐
- Narkasur's wife ☐
- Krishna's wife ☐

Find out

- Now work with a partner.
  Narkasur might have been sorry for more than one reason:
  – because he was dying
  – because his mother was sad
  – because he wanted people to be happy.
- What do you think?
- Talk about each reason with your partner. Can you think of any more?
- Most Hindus believe that a mother's love for her child is pure and can never be wrong.
- How does the story of Krishna and Narkasur show this?
- Was Narkasur really bad or not? What do you think?

Lotus Flower game

Key word answers

2. Samsara/reincarnation
3. Shakti/Durga/Kali
4. Puja
5. Shiva
6. Avatar
7. Samskaras
8. Gandhi (Mahatma)
9. Saraswati
10. Brahma
11. OM
12. Ganesha
13. Vishnu
14. Ramayana
16. Mandir
17. Dharma
19. Karma
20. Krishna
21. Ganges
23. Lakshmi
24. Bhagavad Gita

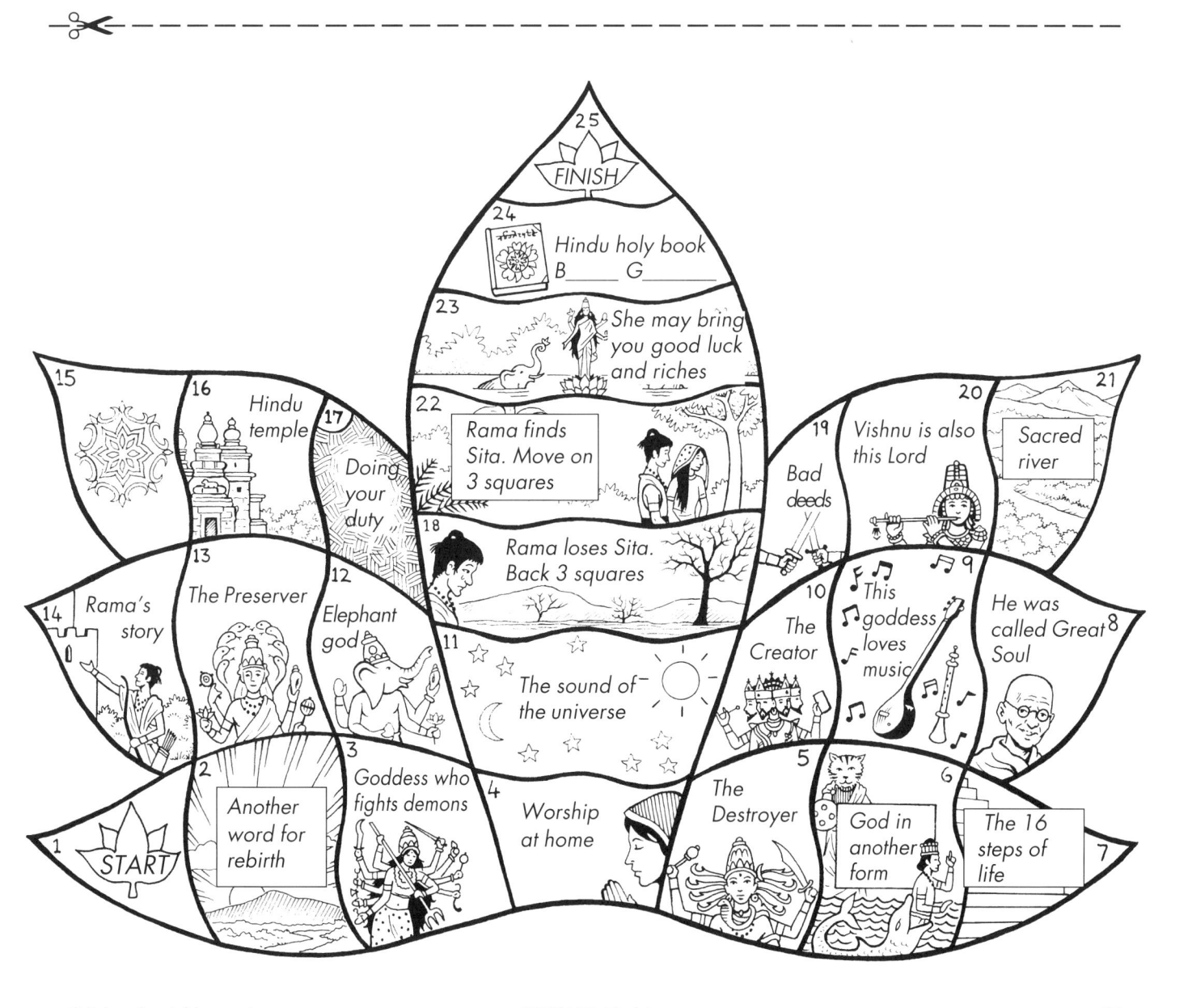

---

25 FINISH

24. Hindu holy book B____ G____

23. She may bring you good luck and riches

22. Rama finds Sita. Move on 3 squares

18. Rama loses Sita. Back 3 squares

15.

16. Hindu temple

17. Doing your duty

20. Vishnu is also this Lord

21. Sacred river

19. Bad deeds

14. Rama's story

13. The Preserver

12. Elephant god

11. The sound of the universe

10. The Creator

9. This goddess loves music

8. He was called Great Soul

2. Another word for rebirth

3. Goddess who fights demons

4. Worship at home

5. The Destroyer

6. God in another form

7. The 16 steps of life

1. START

Glossary

ahimsa – Hindu belief in non-violence.
Arjuna – Prince who appears in the **Bhagavad Gita**.
arranged marriage – where the bride and groom have been chosen by the families.
arti ceremony – daily worship of light at a Hindu temple.
arti lamp – a small lamp containing oil used in worship.
arti tray – used in worship to hold offerings.
Aryans – early people who settled in the Indus valley.
Ashwin – September, October in the Hindu calendar.
atman – the soul.
avatar – a god who comes down to earth in another form.
Bengal – a region of North East India.
Bhagavad Gita – Hindu holy book, part of the **Mahabharata**.
Brahma – the Creator, one of the three main Hindu gods.
Brahmin – a Hindu caste of priests and wise men.
burfi – a Hindu sweet made of milk.
caste – Hindu system splits people into upper and lower classes.
chant – song in one tone, often religious.
chapati – Indian flat bread.
class – people split into upper and lower sections of society.
conch – large sea shell.
cosmic – belonging to the universe.
creation – something that has been made or given life.
cremation – burying of a dead body.
Cycle of Life – Hindu belief in life, death and rebirth.
Dalit – **oppressed**, the poorest people in India.
Dassehra – Hindu festival of the goddess Durga.
deity – god or goddess.
dharma – Hindu's duty in life.
dharmasala – a room used by **pilgrims.**
discus – a round metal plate, can be used as a weapon.
Divali – Hindu festival of lights.
Durga – **Shakti** as a warrior goddess
family tree – a chart which shows family relationships.
festival – a special day when people enjoy themselves.
funeral – when a body is buried or cremated.
Gajamukha – Hindu monster king killed by **Ganesha**.
Gandhi – (**Mohandas**) Hindu who led non-violent protest in India.
Ganesha – Hindu elephant god worshipped when hard task to be done.
Ganesha Chaturthi – Hindu festival for **Ganesha**.
Ganga – goddess of the river **Ganges**.
Ganges – holy river in India.
garland – necklace of flowers.
Garuda – creature, half-man, half-bird.
ghee – Indian butter milk used in cooking.
goblin – demon or evil spirit.
Hanuman – Hindu monkey god, loyal servant of Prince **Rama**.
Harijan – 'children of god' the name given to the **Dalits** by **Gandhi**.
henna – red plant dye.
Himalayas – mountain range running through North India.
Hinduism – the main Indian religion involving reincarnation.
Holi – the Hindu Spring festival.
Holika – female Hindu demon.
horoscope – chart of the planets at the time of a person's birth.
hourglass – a measure of time, sand runs through glass for an hour.
hymn – religious song.
illegal – against the law.
incarnation – appearing in a different form (see **avatar**).
incense – a spice which gives a sweet smell when burned.
Indra – **Aryan** god of heaven and storm.
Indralock – home of the **Aryan** gods.
Indus Valley – valley in North West India.
Janmashtami – festival of **Krishna**'s birthday.
Kali – **Shakti** as goddess of death and destroyer of time.
karma – good or bad results of actions.
Kartik – Hindu god of war, son of **Parvati** and **Shiva**.
kheer – Indian food like rice pudding.
Krishna – an **avatar** of **Vishnu**.
Kshatriya – the Hindu caste of rulers and generals.
Lakshmana – (Prince) **Rama**'s brother.
Lakshmi – goddess of riches and prosperity, **Vishnu's** wife.
Lanka – Sri Lanka, an island off southern India.
Lord of the Dance – **Shiva** as the dancer who keeps the cycle of life, death and rebirth moving.
lotus flower – water lily symbolising beauty, peace and protection.

mace – heavy weapon like a club.
Mahabharata – Hindu holy book which tells of a great battle.
Mahatma – 'great soul', the name given to **Mohandas Gandhi**.
mandap – covering held above bride and groom at a Hindu wedding.
mandir – Hindu temple.
mango – juicy fruit.
meditate – to think or pray silently.
moksha – when the soul is free from rebirth.
Mura – a five-headed monster.
murti – small statue of a Hindu god or goddess.
Narkasur – Hindu giant demon.
Nataraj – Shiva as the cosmic dancer.
Navaratri – festival celebrating goddess Durga.
offerings – a present given to the gods.
OM – the sound which represents creation.
oppressed – treated unfairly.
origin – beginning of something.
Parvati – **Shiva**'s wife, mother of **Ganesh** and **Kartik** (see also **Uma**).
Phalguna – March in the Hindu calendar.
pilgrim – person who makes a journey to a holy place.
pilgrimage – journey made by a pilgrim.
Pole Star – star near the North Pole.
Pongal – cow festival in South India.
prasad – food which has been blessed.
protest – to speak against something.
puja – Hindu act of worship.
Punjab – region of North India.
puri – Indian bread which is fried.
pyre – pile of wood which is burnt in Indian cremation.
quality – what makes a character.
raita – Indian yoghurt.
Raksha Bandhan – Hindu Festival – sisters give their brothers bracelets.
Rama – (Prince) an **avatar** of **Vishnu**.
Rama Naumi – festival of **Rama**'s birthday.
Ramayana – great poem which tells **Rama**'s story.
rangoli – patterns made on ground with coloured powder and sand.
Rath Yatra – Hindu chariot festival.
rebirth – to be born again.
reincarnation – when the soul is reborn in another body (see **samsara**).
religion – system of belief in gods and goddesses.
sacred – holy object.
sacred thread – the tenth **samskara**.
sadhu – Hindu holy man.
samsara – **reincarnation**; when the soul is reborn in another body.
samskara – a step (of which there are sixteen) taken by the **soul**.
Saraswati – Hindu goddess of music and learning, wife of **Vishnu**.
sari – woman's robe wrapped around the body.
Shakti – the main Hindu goddess, wife of **Shiva**.
Shiva – Hindu god, the Destroyer.
Shivatri – festival of the god Shiva.
shrine – a holy place.
shroud – a cloth wrapped around a dead body.
Shudra – the Hindu caste of unskilled workers.
sign –
Sita – **Rama**'s wife.
soul – a person's spirit, believed to continue living after body has died.
Supreme One – the highest being which for Hindus is everything.
symbol – something which represents something else.
tassel – a decoration of hanging threads on a rope of cloth.
temple – place of worship.
tikka mark – tradional red mark on the forehead.
tradition – old customs.
Ugadi – Hindu New Year.
Uma – **Shiva**'s wife, another name for **Parvati.**
universe – all things that exist in the world and throughout space.
Untouchable – a name given to the **Dalits.**
Vaishaya – the Hindu caste of businessmen and skilled workers.
Varanasi – holy city on Ganges
Vedas – ancient Hindu book.
vegetarian – someone who does not eat meat.
verse – line of poem or chant.
Vishnu – Hindu god, the Preserver.
worship – to follow a god.
Yudishthira – a great soldier in the **Mahabharata**.